$$\cos x = \frac{A}{H}$$

$$\tan x = \frac{O}{A}$$

$$\frac{1}{2}x$$

DEMCO

LIGHT
SCIENCE
TRICKS

Library of Congress Cataloging-in-Publication Data

Murray, Peter, 1952 Sept. 29
  Professor Solomon Snickerdoodle's Light Science Tricks / author, Peter
Murray: Penny Dann, illustrator.
    p. cm.
    ISBN 1-56766-148-3
    1. Light—Juvenile literature. 2. Light—Experiments—Juvenile literature.
3. Scientific recreations—Juvenile literature. [1. Light—Experiments.
2. Experiments. 3. Scientific recreations.]
I. Title. II. Title: Light science tricks.
QC360.M88 1998
535'.078—DC20   98-10203
                                                     CIP
                                                     AC

LIGHT SCIENCE TRICKS

With
Professor Solomon
Snickerdoodle
by
Peter Murray

THE INVISIBLE PROFESSOR

I was walking past Professor Solomon Snickerdoodle's place one day, when I noticed a strange cardboard thingamajig sticking up over the top of his fence. When I moved, it followed me!

I guessed right away that the professor was pulling another one of his "science tricks," so I stopped and peered carefully into the open end of the thingamajig. A single eye stared back at me.

I called out, "Is that you, Professor?"

The eye blinked, and a voice came from the other side of the fence. "How did you know?"

"Just a lucky guess," I said. "How did you get your eye into the end of a cardboard thingamajig?"

"Well," said the invisible professor, "I was in my laboratory this morning, bouncing some light around, and the next thing I knew, I could see around corners and over fences! It's really quite astounding. Would you like to try it?"

"Sure," I said. "Why not?" The professor is an odd fellow, but his experiments are usually first rate.

THE PROFESSOR'S PECULIAR PERISCOPE

I walked down the sidewalk to the gate, where I met the professor. He was looking into one end of a long, square cardboard tube.

"A most provocative apparatus," observed the professor, who never misses a chance to misuse a big word. "Have you ever looked into a periscope?"

I shook my head. I thought periscopes had something to do with submarines. I'd never seen one made out of cardboard!

The professor handed the periscope to me. I put my eye to one end of the tube and gasped.

"It's like being seven feet tall!" I exclaimed. I turned the periscope around, then tipped it down and looked into the professor's face. He was smiling.

"It's a simple matter of bouncing the light around, my young friend!"

HOW TO MAKE A PERISCOPE:

Materials

2 small mirrors, about 2 x 3 inches (you can buy them
in most drugstores)

1 large piece of stiff cardboard
(12 by 20 inches)

A sharp utility knife

Tape

Note: Find an adult to help you with the cutting part!

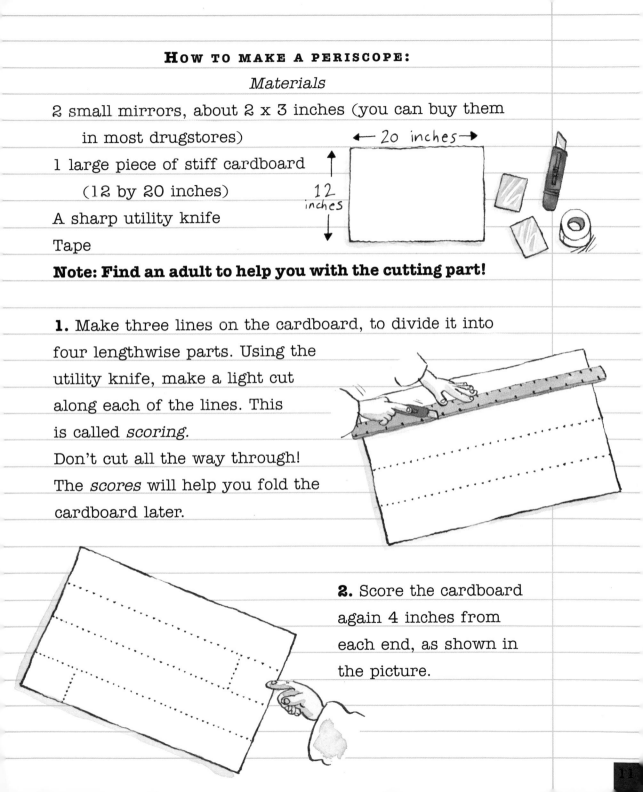

← 20 inches →

12 inches

1. Make three lines on the cardboard, to divide it into
four lengthwise parts. Using the
utility knife, make a light cut
along each of the lines. This
is called *scoring*.
Don't cut all the way through!
The *scores* will help you fold the
cardboard later.

2. Score the cardboard
again 4 inches from
each end, as shown in
the picture.

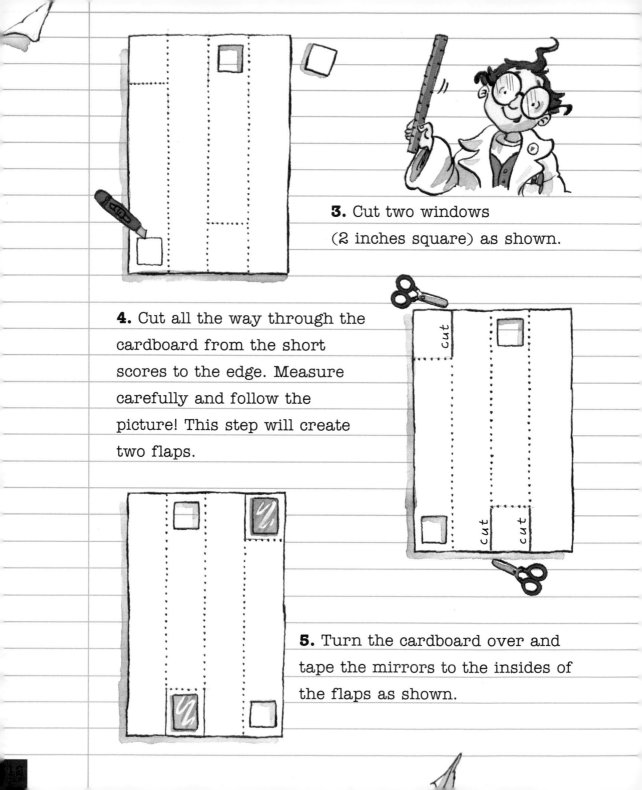

3. Cut two windows (2 inches square) as shown.

4. Cut all the way through the cardboard from the short scores to the edge. Measure carefully and follow the picture! This step will create two flaps.

cut

cut

cut

5. Turn the cardboard over and tape the mirrors to the insides of the flaps as shown.

mirror

window

tape

6. Fold the cardboard into a tube (the mirrors will be on the inside of the tube) and tape it together.

fold in

7. Fold in the flaps until they touch the other side of the tube. Fasten them with tape.

fold in

8. Look through either end of the periscope. What do you see?

NOTE:

If your periscope doesn't work, try adjusting the angle of the flaps.

Periscopes can help you see around corners or over fences. If you are a kid in a crowd of tall adults, you can use your periscope to see over their heads!

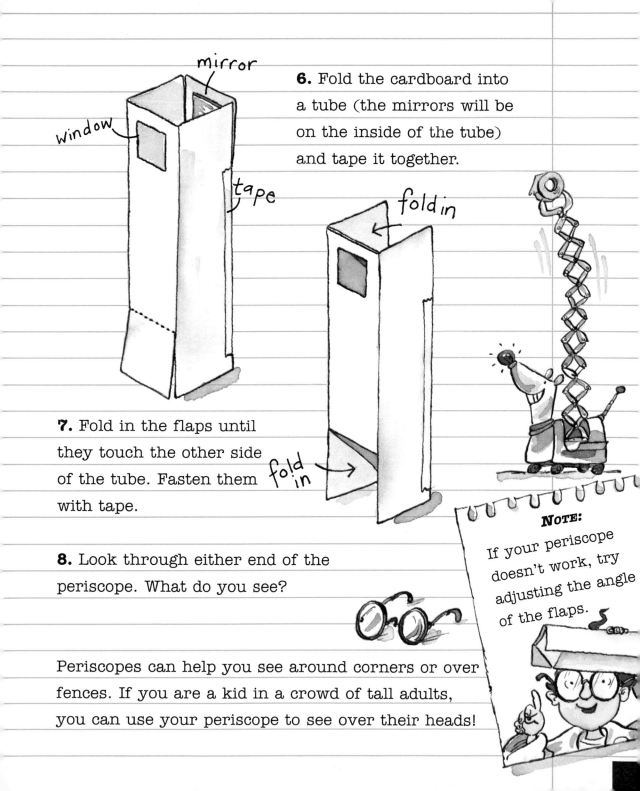

Light enters here - - - - - - - - - - - - - - - ▷

mirror

bounces off mirror, travels through tube, bounces again

How periscopes work:

Periscopes use two carefully positioned mirrors to control light. Light moves in a straight line until it bounces off something. When you look into a mirror, light bounces from your face to the mirror's surface and back again to your eyes. What you see is the *reflection* of the light from your face.

When you stand to one side of a mirror, you can't see yourself because the light bounces off the surface at an angle. By adjusting the angle of a mirror, you can use it to see things that are not directly in front of you. Periscope mirrors are angled so that light bounces off the top mirror, hits the bottom mirror and bounces again, and goes right to your eye. You are seeing the same light that enters the top of the periscope!

card

▷ to me

mirror

I held the periscope up to my eye and used it to look down at the professor.

"Hello down there," I called out.

"Hello yourself," said the professor.

you! ‎--▷

Professor Solomon S

THE PLASTIC LIGHT BENDER

"I should probably tell you," said the professor ponderously, "that bit about light traveling in a straight line is not always precisely absolutely undeniably true. It *is* possible to bend light."

"Bend light? How do you do that?" I imagined it would take some sort of enormous machine. Professor Snickerdoodle stroked his chin. "There are many possibilities. The air we breathe bends light. A magnifying glass bends it even better. Even gravity bends light. My favorite light-bender, however, is a plastic tube. Would you like to go into a dark closet and shut the door?"

If anybody else had asked me that, I would have said "No!" But I knew that the professor only wanted to show me one of his experiments.

HOW TO BEND LIGHT:

You will need a dark room or closet, a flashlight, and 3 feet of clear, flexible plastic tubing.

1. Fasten the tube to the end of the flashlight so the light shines into the open end of the tube. You can use cellophane tape to hold the tube against the flashlight.

2. Run the other end of the tube under the door of a dark room or closet.

3. Turn the flashlight on.

4. Get into the closet and close the door. Look at the end of the plastic tube. What do you see?

HOW IT WORKS:

The light from the flashlight follows the curve of the plastic tubing. Notice that the light doesn't go through the hollow part of the tube, but instead stays in the plastic walls. You can also do this experiment with a solid plastic rod.

This way of controlling light is called *fiber optics*. Light that passes into a clear plastic rod or tube bounces off its surface from the *inside*, forcing the light to follow the plastic around curves, corners, and loop-the-loops. Glass fibers will also transmit light around a curve. Doctors sometimes use long, flexible glass fibers to see inside the human body!

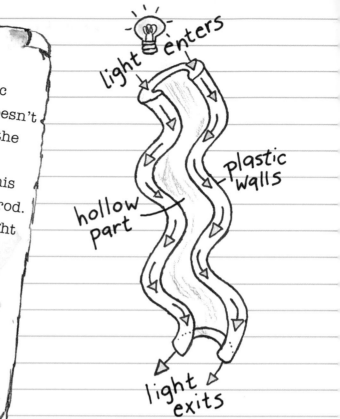

I tried looking into the end of the plastic tube. "So this works something like a periscope? I can't see a thing!"

The professor said, "The principle is similar, but the plastic tube isn't clear enough to transmit a good image. By the time the light gets from one end to the other, it's all busted up and fuzzy."

THE LIGHT BUSTER

"**W**hat do you mean, 'busted up'?" I asked.

"I mean smashed, shattered, splintered, and fractured!" answered the professor. "Have I ever shown you my Light Buster?"

I shook my head. The professor smiled and showed me a small, wedge-shaped chunk of glass.

"That's a light buster?"

"It's better known as a *prism*," said the professor. "Observe!" The professor placed the prism on a sunny windowsill.

"Nothing's happening," I observed.

"Inaccurate and imprecise!" declared the professor. He pointed to a spot on the opposite wall.

"It looks like a little rainbow!" I exclaimed.

Professor Snickerdoodle smiled. "Actually," he said, "what you are seeing is the *spectrum!*"

HOW TO MAKE YOUR OWN PRISM:

You can make a prism using two small mirrors (about 2 inches x 3 inches), a pan full of water, and a sunny day.

1. Fill the pan with water to a depth of 2 inches. Place it in a window so the sun hits it directly.

2. Using small bricks or stones, prop the mirrors up in the pan so that they form a V. The mirrors should be facing each other. Position the mirrors so one of them is facing the sun.

3. Wait for the surface of the water to settle down, then look for the spectrum to appear on your walls or ceiling. If you can't find it, try changing the angle of the mirrors. Once you get the mirrors positioned just right, your prism will start working.

HOW IT WORKS:

When you positioned your mirrors in the water, you created a triangular section of water that works just like a glass prism.

Sunlight is a combination of many different colors of light. The group of colors we can see is called the *visible spectrum*. An apple looks red because its skin reflects only red light. A marshmallow looks white because its surface reflects all the different colors of visible light.

When light passes through a clear substance such as glass or water, it bends. This is called *refraction*. Prisms are triangle-shaped, and when the light passes through such a shape, the different colors are bent by different amounts. The red light bends the least, the purple light bends the most. You can see the separate colors that make white light in the form of a *spectrum*.

A rainbow is a special kind of spectrum that occurs when sunlight passes through water droplets high in the air.

THE SNICKERDOODLE SPINNER

"**N**ow that we've broken light into its different colors, I'll show you how to reverse the process. All we have to do is mix the colors together and we'll see white light!"

"You mean mix up a bunch of paint colors?"

"No, no, no! We want to mix the colored *light*, not paint! If you just stir a bunch of paint together you will get a color called YECCH!"

"Is 'YECCH' one of your scientific words?" I asked.

"No. But it's a very good word to know." The professor opened one of his many drawers and pulled out a cardboard disk with colors painted on the sides. A long loop of string was strung through holes in the center of the disk.

"As you can see," said the professor, "the disk is painted red, yellow, and blue. Now observe what happens when I start it spinning!"

The professor put one hand in each end of the loop, and the disk began to spin. At first, I could see the colors going around and around, but as the disk went faster, the colors suddenly disappeared! The disk had turned pure white!

How to Make a Snickerdoodle Spinner:

1. Cut a disk 6 inches in diameter from a piece of heavy cardboard that is white on one side. (If the cardboard isn't white, glue a sheet of white paper to one side.)

2. Punch two holes in the cardboard, ½ inch apart, on each side of the center.

3. Divide the white side of the disk into three equal parts. Paint the parts red, yellow, and blue as shown. It's important to make the colors as close to the picture as possible—if they are too dark, the experiment won't work!

4. Run a piece of string through the holes and tie it into a loop.

5. To get the spinner spinning, put one end of the loop around each hand, wind up the disk so the string is all twisted around itself, then slowly pull your hands apart. The disk should start to spin. When you can't pull your hands apart any more, relax and let the disk rewind the string. It might take a little practice, but you'll soon have it going!

HOW IT WORKS:

When the colored disk spins, your eyes aren't fast enough to see the separate colors as they move around in a circle. Instead, you see all three colors at the same time. Red, blue, and yellow light combines to make white light. When you see them all at once, the colors seem to disappear! Try making spinners with other color combinations and patterns. What happens when you use blue and yellow?

6. Now watch what happens to the colored side of the disk. Where do the colors go?

STRAWBERRIES FROM THE SUN

After the spinner experiment,
Professor Snickerdoodle and I sat
on his front steps eating apples.

"Did you know that without light,
you would not be ingesting that apple?" the professor
asked. I looked at the apple. Was I *ingesting* it? What a
terrible thought!

The professor could see he had me confused.
"What I mean," he explained, "is that you would not be
eating it."

"Why? Because I couldn't see it?"

"No! Because without sunlight, there would be no
apples to eat! Let me show you my plant experiment."

The professor took me back to his garden and showed me a healthy green strawberry plant that had one big red strawberry. Beside it sat an upside-down cardboard box.

"What a fine-looking strawberry!" I said.

"Unquestionably!" replied the professor.

"But look at what has happened to its twin!" He lifted the cardboard box. Underneath it, there was a droopy, sick-looking, yellow strawberry plant with no strawberries on it.

The professor explained, "Two weeks ago, these two plants were exactly alike. But when I put the box over one of the plants, I cut off its sunlight. Without light, it could not grow."

WHY PLANTS NEED LIGHT:

Inside the leaves of green plants, a special chemical process called *photosynthesis* takes place. Photosynthesis combines light energy with air and water to create growth. Without light, plants grow limp and yellow and eventually die.

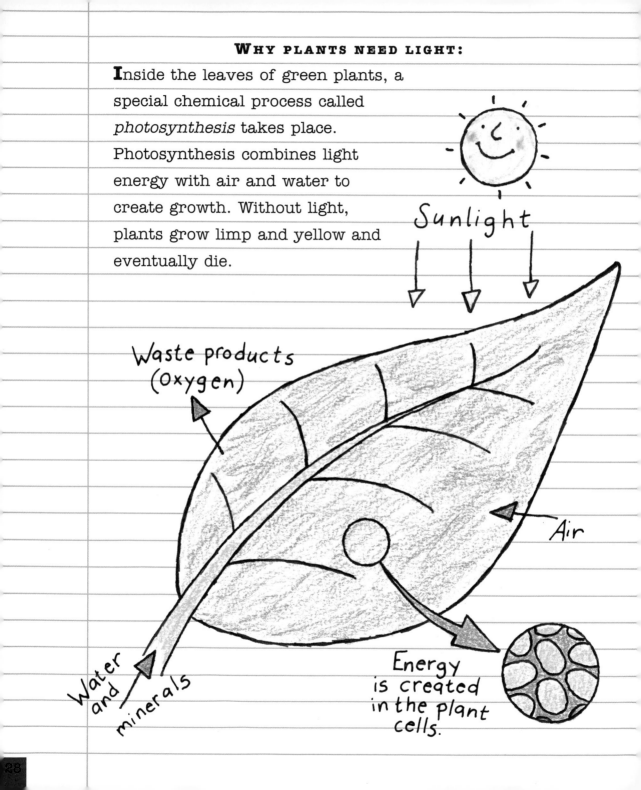

Sunlight

Waste products (Oxygen)

Air

Water and minerals

Energy is created in the plant cells.

I picked the strawberry from the healthy plant, then looked down at the sickly yellow plant. "What a terrible thing to do to a strawberry plant!" I said.

"We'll leave the box off," said the professor. "Perhaps the plant will recover."

"Next time you do this experiment, you should use a *broccoli* plant," I said.

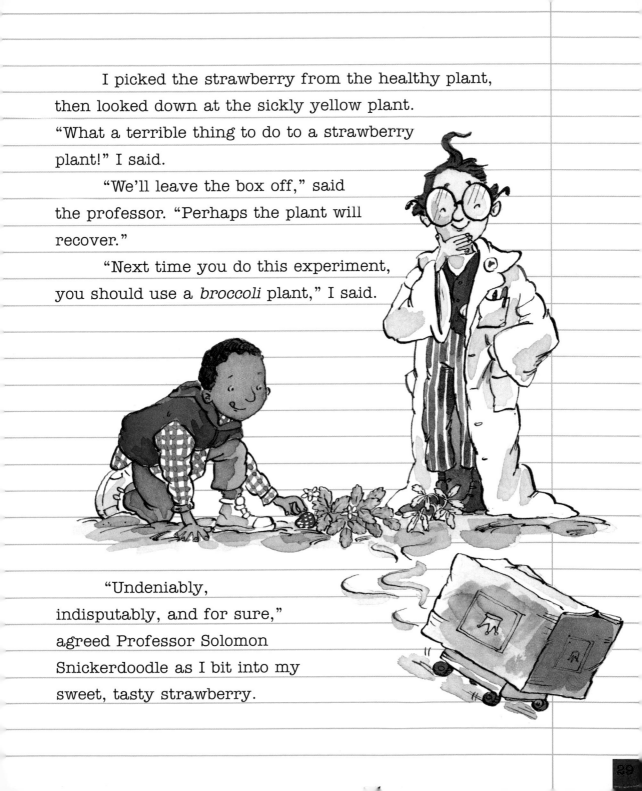

"Undeniably, indisputably, and for sure," agreed Professor Solomon Snickerdoodle as I bit into my sweet, tasty strawberry.

$E = mc^2$

$$\frac{\begin{array}{r} 11 \\ \times 5 \end{array}}{55}$$

$a^2 + b^2 = c^2$

$\frac{1}{2} bh$ = area of triangle